EXCAVATORS

by Aubrey Zalewski

Cody Koala

An Imprint of Pop!
popbooksonline.com

abdobooks.com
Published by Pop!, a division of ABDO, PO Box 398166, Minneapolis, Minnesota 55439. Copyright © 2020 by POP, LLC. International copyrights reserved in all countries. No part of this book may be reproduced in any form without written permission from the publisher. Pop!™ is a trademark and logo of POP, LLC.

Printed in the United States of America, North Mankato, Minnesota

052019
092019

THIS BOOK CONTAINS
RECYCLED MATERIALS

Cover Photo: Shutterstock Images
Interior Photos: Shutterstock Images 1; iStockphoto, 5, 7 (top), 7 (bottom left), 7 (bottom right), 9, 10–11, 12, 15, 16, 18, 19, 20–21

Editor: Meg Gaertner
Series Designer: Sophie Geister-Jones

Library of Congress Control Number: 2018964595
Publisher's Cataloging-in-Publication Data
Names: Zalewski, Aubrey, author.
Title: Excavators / by Aubrey Zalewski.
Description: Minneapolis, Minnesota : Pop!, 2020 | Series: Construction vehicles | Includes online resources and index.
Identifiers: ISBN 9781532163326 (lib. bdg.) | ISBN 9781644940051 (pbk.) | ISBN 9781532164767 (ebook).
Subjects: LCSH: Excavation--Juvenile literature. | Construction equipment--Juvenile literature. | Construction industry--Equipment and supplies--Juvenile literature.
Classification: DDC 629.225--dc23

Hello! My name is

Cody Koala

Pop open this book and you'll find QR codes like this one, loaded with information, so you can learn even more!

Scan this code* and others like it while you read, or visit the website below to make this book pop.

popbooksonline.com/excavators

*Scanning QR codes requires a web-enabled smart device with a QR code reader app and a camera.

Table of Contents

The Excavator Can Help!

An old building needs to be torn down. An excavator pulls down pieces of the building. Then it picks up the mess.

Watch a video here!

An Excavator's Job

Excavators do many different jobs. They dig holes for roads and buildings. They dig in **mines**. Excavators also knock down buildings and trees.

Learn more here!

Parts of an Excavator

An excavator moves on **tracks**. The driver sits in the **cab**. The driver controls the excavator's movement.

> The cab can spin in a complete circle.

The **boom** sticks out from the cab. It moves up and down. The boom ends at a **joint**.

The joint connects
the boom to an arm.
The arm moves forward
and backward.

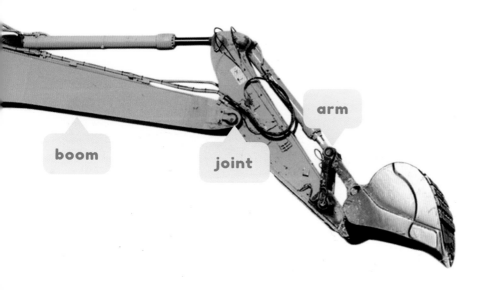

boom

joint

arm

The arm connects the boom and the **bucket**. The bucket can dig, push, or scrape. Buckets come in many shapes and sizes.

Excavators are also called diggers.

Chapter 4

Types of Excavators

There are many types of excavators. Some excavators have extra-long arms and **booms**. These excavators can reach far.

Learn more here!

joint

Other excavators have booms with more **joints**. These booms are called knuckle booms. They can move up and down and left to right.

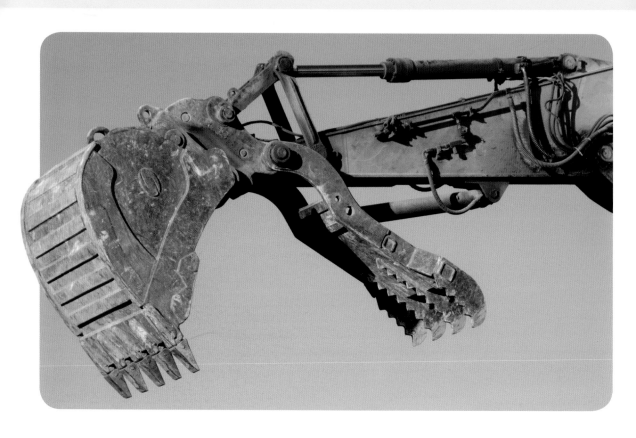

Excavators are not just used for digging. A **grapple** might replace the **bucket**.

grapple

The grapple can grab and lift things. It is also useful for tearing things down.

Some excavators have different **tracks**. A swamp excavator's tracks are wide.

The tracks are also bigger than usual. They help the excavator float on water.

Making Connections

Text-to-Self

Have you ever seen an excavator? What was it doing? If you haven't seen one, where might you see one?

Text-to-Text

Have you read about another construction vehicle? How is it similar to or different from an excavator?

Text-to-World

Different excavators are best for different jobs. How do other tools match their jobs?

Glossary

boom – a long arm that sticks out from an excavator's base.

bucket – the part of an excavator that digs into the ground.

cab – the part of an excavator where the driver sits.

grapple – a tool used to grab or lift things.

joint – the point that connects two parts of an excavator.

mine – a place where people dig up minerals.

track – one of two metal belts on the bottom of an excavator that help it move.

Index

Online Resources

popbooksonline.com

Thanks for reading this Cody Koala book!

Scan this code* and others like it in this book, or visit the website below to make this book pop!

popbooksonline.com/excavators

*Scanning QR codes requires a web-enabled smart device with a QR code reader app and a camera.